Into a
Land of
Strangers

Library and Archives Canada Cataloguing in Publication

Title: Into a land of strangers / John B. Lee.

Other titles: Poems. Selections

Names: Lee, John B., 1951- author.

Description: Poems.

Identifiers: Canadiana (print) 20190043733 | Canadiana (ebook) 20190043741 | ISBN 9781771614436 (softcover) | ISBN 9781771614443 (HTML) | ISBN 9781771614450 (Kindle) | ISBN 9781771614467 (PDF)

Classification: LCC PS8573.E348 A6 2019 | DDC C811/.54—dc23

Published by Mosaic Press, Oakville, Ontario, Canada, 2019.

MOSAIC PRESS, Publishers
Copyright © John B. Lee, 2019

Cover desing by Brianna Wodabek

ONTARIO ARTS COUNCIL
CONSEIL DES ARTS DE L'ONTARIO
an Ontario government agency
un organisme du gouvernement de l'Ontario

We acknowledge the Ontario Arts Council
for their support of our publishing program

Funded by the Government of Canada
Financé par le gouvernement du Canada

MOSAIC PRESS
1252 Speers Road, Units 1 & 2
Oakville, Ontario L6L 5N9
phone: (905) 825-2130

info@mosaic-press.com

Into a
Land of
Strangers

John B. Lee

You cannot write my poems
Just as I cannot dream your dreams.

From "Dream and Poetry" by Chinese poet Hu Shih

for my great-aunt Ida Wight nee Emerick

elementary schoolteacher in Canada
missionary and school superintendent in China

Poems from **Into a Land of Strangers** have been published in the website Numero Cinq, Dieresis: Revista de Arte y Literatura, translated into Spanish for publication in Cuba, Big Pond Rumours E zine anthology, The Great American Wiseass Poetry anthology, Adam and Eve & the Riders of the Apocalypse anthology, the anthology Family Ties: Memories, Poetry and Good Food, Quills, Latchkey, The Saving Banister, The Literary Connection, Volume 2: My Canada, Volume 3: Lest We Forget, Niagara Poetry Anthology, Volume 29, the anthology Scarlet Thistles, Synaresis, Voices Israel 2014, Wax Poetry & Art International★ (these poems were acknowledged as the fourth most visited poems in the site), Windsor Review, 50+ Poems for Gordon Lightfoot, and Lummox magazine

the poem "The Great Wall of China," received the Literary Encyclopedia Award, and has been nominated for a Pushcart Poetry Award by Hourglass, "The insatiable hungers of the sun," received second place honours in the Scugog Council for the Arts poetry competition for 2014, and the suite of poems under the working title "Counting Cranes" received first honourable mention in the Cranberry Tree press chapbook awards for 2015 and in the Big Pond Rumours chapbook awards of 2017 and were republished in the book This is How We See the World, Hidden Brook Press, 2018

Table of Contents

Let Loose the Dogs of Peace: the life and times of
Ida Wight nee Emerick   xv

Part I--Into a Land of Strangers

The life a woman makes   1

Wine and bread   12

?   14

The Impossible Black Tulip   15

Celestial China   18

Into a Land of Strangers   20

Maiden/Bride/Mother/Widow/Refugee   23

Wedding Photo, Chi Nan Fu China Mission, December 7, 1897   26

is not this ... (a Haibun)   29

When Shining Dreams   35

A Person on Business from Porlock   36

She Performs   39

Reveal   41

Considering Ancient Chinese Erotica   43

The Superintendent   45

At Least for Now 48

Foreign Devil 50

Snow: translation of a poem by Mao Tse Tung 53

So the Story Goes 54

Hussies Don't Wear Girdles, Girls 62

Now and Then 64

In the basement of the Mary Webb Centre 66

I handle your sent-home silks 66

The Rape of Nanking 70

Via Dolorosa: from a Photograph Taken on Bloody Saturday During the Battle of Shanghai 78

Black Christmas 80

Thus the Wild Fox 83

Our Own Particular Time 85

Send Me the Names 88

The Importance of 'The' 90

Because She Failed to Attend Her Sister's Anniversary 92

The Blue and Boundless Cage of Paradise 94

Part II--Counting Cranes

Mu—Not—lament for the lost kingdom of I am 99

A dream I dream on my first night in Beijing 102

Is Beijing burning 103

A boy speaks of his childhood in the countryside outside of Beijing 105

Undeserving blue 107

Tea flower falling   109

Climbing the Great Wall of China   111

Counting cranes   113

The empty boat   116

The Chinese on the moon   117

I thought I was in China held against my will   118

Suseok—viewing stones   119

An incident at the bridge of no return   122

The outset   124

Timmy's down the well   126

Broken time traveller   129

The insatiable hungers of the sun   131

Last night we were speaking of spiders   133

Going back to the world   135

Afterword

Let Loose the Dogs of Peace: the life and
times of Ida Wight nee Emerick
(1867–1951)

Better to be a dog in a time of peace,
than to be human in a time of war
1627 Feng Menglong

I was born into a family of bibliophiles. The bookcase located in the upstairs hallway outside my bedroom represented the accumulation of four generations of readers. Those bookshelves contained an eclectic collection ranging from animal husbandry to Victorian poetry, from bodice rippers to philosophical tracts, from tomes of scientific speculation to dithyrambs of evangelical proselytizing. Billy Sunday sat beside Spinoza. Einstein leaned against Longfellow. *A Breeder's Guide to Lincoln Long Wool Sheep* grazed the shelf next to *A Boy's Own Encyclopedia.*

Ever a bookish lad, the first hint of a family connection to China goes to my discovery of two smallish volumes bound in faded blue linen end boards held fast by eye-hooked ivory needles laced through stays set in the left-hand spine, the books in question held closed as though boxed for shipping. The front covers were bedizened by a single line of Chinese characters displaying the exotic logograms of the realm of the Han. But when I discovered those books I was a preliterate lad, and so for me, these characters were no less mysterious than the alphabet I would come to learn.

On the inside cover of both of those blue-linen volumes, a younger version of myself seems to have laid claim to the texts.

My name appears there on the book flap printed in blunt primary school pencil, the 'h' truncated and thus barely distinguishable from the 'n', the L squat beside the overgrown squiggle of a pair of 'e's' making it obvious that I was in dire need of instruction and careful guidance concerning my preschooler's penmanship. In addition to these incompetently rendered identifiers, it seems I was attempting the squiggle of a scribbler's cursive, my callow hand having mastered something of a wavy line like a cross between a cardiogram and the roiling surface of a windy lake.

The books themselves are composed of ink drawing and Chinese characters scribed on page after page of time-yellowed rice paper stitched into three separate gatherings. I suspect that the content might be something of botanical interest, since the ink drawings represent delicately rendered cherry blossoms and cut bamboo sketched against a backdrop of mountains and rivers.

★

Since about age ten I'd known that I had a great-aunt who had served as a missionary in China. Around the same time as the sale of the farm in the late autumn of 2008, I began to entertain the idea of writing something about this great-aunt. I knew her name was Ida, and that she was somehow related to my paternal grandmother, though I didn't know much else. Somewhere in the back of my mind I seemed to recall that Aunt Ida's daughter Frances had been bridesmaid at my paternal grandparents' wedding in 1910. I'd written a book about my grandmother Stella published in 1999. It would involve another fifteen years of maturing as a writer before it occurred to me to return to that fertile ground and to tell the story of grandma's aunt Ida. *Where might I start?* With Stella I had begun my research by interviewing those who had known her well and by looking at photographs. I had no photographs of Ida and I knew no one with a living memory of her life.

When it comes to genealogy, I have always been fortunate. I am fifth generation born and raised on the farm established by my great-great grandfather and namesake John Lee. And I have the blessing of having two cousins and a mother with an enthusiasm for ancestral research. My cousin Dorothy Lee Kay, daughter to my father's sister Emily, has done extensive research into the lives of all of our shared ancestors, and her work has yielded a very copious and finely detailed account of the life of Ida Jean Wight nee Emerick. And it was she who provided the lion's share of primary information that became the seedbed of my book *Into a Land of Strangers*. And it was she who packaged up and sent me the aforementioned blue linen books rescued from the library in the hall on the farm. I am now in possession of those books that most certainly must have come to the farm from aunt Ida given as gifts to her niece, my grandmother Stella.

Thanks to cousin Dorothy's meticulous genealogy, I have been able to fix essential dates for Ida's life and times set against a backdrop of history.

★

Born in the year of Canada's confederation, December 17th 1867, in Waterford, Ontario Ida Jean Emerick's life might be described as being lived according to the apocryphal Chinese curse *may you live in interesting times*. Her paternal grandfather Francis Emerick, a late-come loyalist of German stock immigrating from New York State into Upper Canada circa 1800, had lost his health and the vigor of his youth fighting on behalf of the British cause as a private in the Lincoln militia during the winter campaigns of the War of 1812. His son, Ida's father John, having served briefly as a travelling Methodist minister died tragically in his thirty-second year due to complications resulting from an injury suffered at a logging bee, thereby leaving seven-year-old Ida and her nine-year-old sister Mara (my great-grandmother) fatherless. However, their mother Elizabeth would remarry several times before passing away in 1928.

After completing normal school, Ida Emerick became a teacher in Highgate Public School SSNo12, where she taught my great-aunt Mary. She went from there to become principal of Essex Public School and then in 1892 at the age of twenty-five she joined the China Inland Mission. First she travelled to the city of Chi-Nan-Fu, and from there to Teng-Chow-Fu, both located in the Shandong province of northeast China. On December 7th 1897 she married fellow missionary the Reverend Calvin Wight. They took up residence in Chi-Nan Fu where she served as a teacher in the missionary school. Their only child Frances was born in December 1898, and seven months later Ida's husband Calvin died on pneumonia July 13th, 1899 four months shy of the outbreak known as the Boxer Rebellion. It is difficult not to infer that his health was compromised by the turbulent times leading up to the outbreak of the peasant uprising. The Boxer Rebellion was a violent anti-foreign and anti-Christian uprising that took place in China between 1899 and 1901. Given the fact that as a missionary it was not safe for her to remain in China, Ida, with her baby girl in her arms, walked across China to Korea and from there to the boats that would carry them to home to America. During this trek she suffered the privations of the refugee and according to private accounts "having such terrible pain and cramps, she put something ... anything into her body giving her baby daughter the same boiled water to ease her pain." She remained in the bosom of family for two years before returning to China, order having been restored and the rebellion having been quelled in that troubled nation.

Her home in Chi-Nan-Fu having been totally destroyed, she relocated to Tang-Chow-Fu where she and her daughter Frances took up residence and after working as principal at a girl's school, she was promoted to Inspector of Schools for the entire region. Frances married Calvin Cook circa 1925 residing with her husband in the European enclave of Shanghai where she gave birth to four sons and two daughters.

The Japanese invaded Manchuria in 1931. By 1933 Ida's daughter and three of her six grandchildren were living in the Japanese internment camp in Shanghai. Having left her home Ida was interned in Hong Kong from 1933 until liberation in March of 1936. She wrote on the occasion of her release "Truce today - the wind was contrary, tempestuous. Jesus walked on the China Sea. The wind ceased - There is now calm." She addressed these words in a letter received by my uncle John sealed in an envelope dated May 12th, 1937. Having been liberated from internment in 1938 daughter Frances and family arrived in New York. Ida immigrated to Durban, South Africa where she lived for the remainder of her life until her death on January 1st 1951.

★

In doing research for this book, in addition to reading and gleaning important details from my cousin Dorothy's genealogical records, I read dozens of books on China including revisiting Chinese poetry in translation through several anthologies. I read seminal books on Chinese thought such as *The I Ching, The Little Red Book of Chairman Mao, Thoughts and Quotations of Confuscious,* dozens of books on the opium wars, the Boxer Rebellion, autobiographies by missionaries in China and in 2015 my wife and I travelled to

China where we visited several cities touring the Forbidden City and walking a short distance along the Great Wall. In addition to touring China we have sojourned with my son who lived for a decade in Seoul, Korea thereby giving us a taste of life in the Far East. While we were in the orient we spent a week in a remote region of Thailand. In "Counting Cranes," which constitutes the closing section of *Into a Land of Strangers,* the reader will find the poems I wrote while travelling in China and Korea.

The final poem in this book makes reference to stones gathered from the muddy bottom of the Mekong River by my younger son who visited Thailand on his honeymoon with his Thai bride Bo. He fell into the water in a shallow region of the river and as he did so he recalled how his father had requested that he bring home rocks for his collection. Those smooth brown stones have joined pebbles from the walls of the palace of Korea, gravel from Tiananmen Square, chips from the Great Wall, scree from the foot of Yanshan Mountains, and rubble from the foot of Gwanaksan in Seoul. I stand firmly by the closing words of that poem which takes its title "Going Back to the World," from the words spoken by American soldiers returning home from Vietnam after their tour of duty.

his father
wants only
the privately precious dross
something marked by the local light
and culled
for lack of beauty but for this:
it was there
in the footstep darkness
of an all-ancestoring night
when empire rose and fell

to the silk breath of a dying counterpane
with maidens gathered in dew

my son knows
his father to be
just the sort of simple man
who like everyone
with a palm line
open to the alms of dawn
might wonder
at want and worth

May 13, 2017

the life a woman makes

★

born a girl

your father took his vows
and stood
looming over the pews
too tall for the pulpit
carpenters lowered
the platform so stepping up
and then down
as though into a well
he stood
hovering over the congregation
like a white-winged
bird of prey

★★

when your papa died
after an accident in the forest
your mother widowed
you and your sister
suddenly fatherless
as you lived there then
sorrowing on the cusp
of first menses
three women
in a manless house
you mourned the loss
though the consolation
of faith
gave sorrow meaning
the midnight over-souled with stars

you might trace
the light of evening
with the delicate
crescent of a cuticle moon

the breath of prayer
that fogs all winter glass
with human frost

a child's prayer
wonders at the proof of dreams

"if I should die before I wake"

your small face drifting
like a cloud
among the pretty constellations
of a golden sky

you'll wear the silver mask of heaven
like a mirror
in a room of light

★★★

the girl you were aspires
among maps and globes
and oraries
and shelves of books
to the ramrod rectitude
of chalk on slate

she does not comprehend
the bullyboys
the flirts and grubby
nosewinds
jostling like pencils spilled
in the wait lines
at the door

come tumbling in
over the trip sill
with hard-packed
ice-dipped, grey-white
winter weaponry
shaping snow
to pack a classmate's
spine-chilled shirt
or flang
the bone orb of a blinking
eye to smarten up the afternoon
with blur and sting

she sits and clicks her shoes
to count

and like a marionette
her hand leaps up and up
as though
delighted by a twitching string

her only mischief
is the secret mirth
she feels
when bad boys
suffer the strap
putting on a brave show

their hot palms red as ochre
as they return to sniffle at their desks
pretending to be careless
as the tear wells
fill to hate the world where teachers live
in the chin tremble
that betrays them to be watched
and she
in her two good shoes
shaping her letters
with greatest care, she colours
within the lines
and reads aloud
to mock the follow finger plods
with her speed

to school to school she seems to say
with every breath
and bell

★★★★

the past must disappear
as warmth through mist
becomes a clarifying blur
of cooling light
both light and vapor mutable in memory
with vanishing transformed
by thought recalled
while every moment blooms
from grey supposes
into blue surmise
where time makes old thread
stronger from the new

the present
burns like sunlit chrome
a brilliant
blindness flashing
in the mind
too bright to see
or seen as fire
sees its fuel in flame
and ashes
heat and dust
as with the wind's result
a fragrant dissipation
made pungent furthest from the source

the future's
like a water moon
where light lies

twice removed
in mysteries of deep
refraction
tilted by a shaded stone
transfixed in motion
like white-washed granite in the sky
the pond's companion
and the well's true friend
as from a luminescent cup
what draws us
to the thirst for light
like darkness drawn
from caverns in the earth
that shimmering quicksilvers in the heart
like prayer
or shimmers at the palm line
with the pulse brushed blue
by language
when we say our dreams aloud

three times
the circle turns
about itself

oh my most repetitious heart's
blue rivers blushing red
returning blue

and as the sky responds to dusk
with its slow startlement of stars
vast whisperings of light

illuminate the spirit
glanced by grace
my sweet companion
my individuated soul
my body sings
in fractions of forever
a song of arrows
breaking into quiet fragments with a wounded voice

★★★★★

the lip of your vulva
milky with semen
you lie in your married bed
wedded to that moment
when in the post-coital night
your womb weeps inward
seeping with the quickening
swim of ovum-piercing
spermatozoa
you almost feel
the sweet conception
of the moon's meiosis
where mutable life
clings to your uterine wall
and after first flowering
you swell in the belly
like summer fruit
caught in the branches of your thighs
you grow heavy
umbilical with heartbeat
throbbing in the chord and then
the fluttery blink of tiny hands
this being the best result
of practised pleasure
you are creatured by love
at the labial crowning
of your baby girl
her new mouth
the warm well of her mammalian thirst
she suckles

and so commences
as with the pulsing of her tongue
she drinks
blue moonlight from dark water

in less than one year
your young husband
will begin his death
and you will flee from China
under the pneumococcal pall
of violent grief
chased by the xenophobic and murderous Boxers
cruel in the city
your house thronging with flowers of fire

you strive to walk
as you starve
and go dry breasted
all this suffering
endured as with the voice of faith
you travel a five-noun journey
virgin, wife, lover, mother, widow
all lived in the lapse of eight brief seasons
two liturgical white-candle winters
and the wine breath
of sorrowful spring
you sojourn in your sister's house in the village
in Canada
your little cherub
toddling into language
and worshipful sunlight

you return to the missionary life in the Orient
taking the slow boat
across the long fever
out of San Francisco
you begin again
becoming someone
you have longed to become
building an old life
defying feng shui
with your home overlooking the water
living there until the Japanese invasion
when that life would collapse again
into the crimson chaos of Bushido and war
under the menses-red Helios of an enemy flag
burning like fire through silk

Wine and bread

you've come to this land
with the words
we say
in service
one woman walking the narrow way
in search
of foreign conversion
the proselytizer
with holy ink on her tongue
like the child
who sucks her pen in school
or a lad who gnaws his pencil to the lead
much like a priest
who cleans his teeth
with twigs of cherry wood
what worries of the world
we feel—come comforted by death
come solve all poverty
in overcrowded hungers
with soft shod throngs
of pig-tailed masses
mastered by a European face
the pedagogue
of simple souls who see
how the green and shallow Jordan
of a water faith
might thread though sorrows
of the sad Yangtze
like the mending of a tailor's hand
five thousand years

of yellow silt in silken seams of Loess
that flood the seasons of the sea
with raptures of the west
and everywhere the blue voice of the sky
follows the cuticle moon in dutiful plods along a line of print
to give the language of the lip
a sacramental metaphor
with letters out of Agamemnon's lexicon
and Latin phrases out of Claudius's stuttering mouth
with doxologies of Albion kings
and American slang to opiate
a sacred breath with wine and bread

?

What is this to me —?
this shadow of the dead
when sorrow
has its long dry season
and we consider without grief
the deeper knowledge of voluminous dust
where the breath of the world
is all there is
to swell the ashen blouse
of earth upon a sun-blackened lawn
where trees
outlive their leaves
a thousand years
I feel this weakening of ink
in ancient lamentations
of a poet's woe
weeping over his lost child
to hear the sob of words
in anthological darkness
where pages press their water marks
to kiss
beneath the paper's weight of shade

The Impossible Black Tulip

*"The men of old see not the moon
  of today; yet the moon of today
  is the moon that shone on them."
    Chinese proverb*

I wonder, Ida
when you joined the mission bound for China
did you know the name
Matteo Ricci, the Jesuit priest
from Italy
the man the Chinese still call
"the scholar from the west"
a sixteenth century Catholic polymath
wearing the robes of a Buddhist monk
impressing the mandarins
of the Ming
mastering the culture and
language of the middle kingdom
and then, mapping the world beyond the world
tracing coastlines on the impossible black tulip
of cartography wherever Magellan sailed
and Columbus lost his way
where the Portuguese, the Spanish, the French
the English, the Dutch
went warring for land
and the madness of gold
and the minds
of the savage
and the bodies of slaves

the rivalries of red-haired kings
and red-robed churches
barbarians and buccaneers uncouth humans
—in the era of inquisition
after Copernicus spun the globe
and Galileo gave heaven away for fear of burning alive
and there the new lands were named
even the home of your birth Ji nádá
first named and thereby known
by the learned classes
who opened their eyes to the west
and the faith of the west
inscribed with the allegory of the Holy Land
and he, the first westerner
to enter into
the Forbidden City
died a failure to evangelize
though he built a cathedral
in the capital
and still, long after
the gunboats have fallen silent
and the opium wars
have burned away
and the Boxers razed
your home and murdered your kind, and the Japanese
imprisoned you and your children
for the sins of empire—his name
lives on
in reverence—
like Li Po's drowning moon
held loose

and glowing in the drunkard's palm
of a midnight pond
the one we might see
if we dare to dream
of a darkness yet to come

Celestial China:

A contemplation on the first recorded appearance of Haley's Comet in a document called 'The Silk Atlas' nearly three thousand years ago ...

the ancient Chinese astronomer
scribes a comet onto silk
the hand that understands the eye
then lifts away
from trails of light
he's seen
as set in ink
upon the shiny worm-work
of his woven cloth

he's satisfied
with proof of mind

the mystery of heaven's
ice and dust a single
wave that breaks upon the roiling sea the breath of wind
that briefly stirs one leaf
a bead of dew
that bends a solitary
blade of grass
and silvers on the green
in spheres that warm and vanish
into nothing much but this--

the silence
after life
that teaches thus

the moon reflects the sun
the river
sees the moon and flows away
as sunlight binds the stars
in all subsuming blue
and we regard
our life
like mirrors of the dead
that hold the face until the light is gone

Into a Land of Strangers

★

the muddy root
of the lotus, also

desires the sky

★

tropical lotus
blooms in the night

white flesh a white moon dreams

★

black water, blue sky
two minds

consider one light

★

undulating cutwater
darkens beneath

the white of a single cloud

★

the lotus open
in the moon-wane of morning

how young a fading white

★

how might the lotus thirst
in the ever-evaporate black

of a deep pool

★

into a land of strangers
she comes

a stranger to herself

★

in the seed pearl
of her beloved moon

the sand grain of her soul

★

celestial stranger
your secret revealed
to a secret concealed
★

an unpainted lotus
imagines the mind

wet brush dampens dry water

★

here in the seam of true silk
the chrysalis clings

to the force of an unborn wing

Maiden / Bride / Mother / Widow / Refugee

not long in the land of strangers
you took the hand
of a missionary man
married into the faith from faith
and soon received his holy seed
in the silken circle of your bridal womb
conceiving a daughter out of love
as you were also
a daughter of Eve
your child born in wedlock
baptized in the first month
of the last year
of the century over a century ago
you were widowed
that same summer
your husband dying
at the time of the upraised hand
of the *righteous hand of harmony*
who hated
the Gwailo
the white ghost of the golden mountain
the westerner sai yan
come to convert and improve
the lot of the lowly and the poor

and how did you see yourself
young mother
in flight under a flag of war
a despised survivor

starving in the kill zone
of a hostile land
your brave body
weakening as you walk
your baby girl
thinning in your embrace
held shadow close as she was
to the milk-drought of your dry breast
you drank ditch water
boiled raw cotton and boot leather for soup

what can we know
of such suffering, we live
on the black-bowelled earth
in the opium darkness
of all similar star-ruined night
when we hunger for sleep
and the human bloom of common dream

at what hour
do we hear
the pharaoh's rage
in the wheel-cut water of a mythic sea
the long nail
fighting the wrist
at the pulse point of a dying god
the Cossack unhorsed
in the red winter of a doomed Shtetl

what might we abhor
and what adore

in us God sees
the season of two fires
and in that second darkness
seems to forge through falsities of time
an afterlife for long-dead stars
that fool us with an ancient light

(*Dec. 7, 1897 married the reverend Calvin Wight/ Dec. 1898 gave birth to daughter Frances, baptized Jan. 17, 1898/ July 13, 1899 widowed during the Boxer Rebellion—fled China on foot*)

Wedding Photo, Chi Nan Fu China Mission, December 7, 1897

the bridal party garbed in unfashionable black
eight deaths ago—
two girls in gloves
one standing at a cant on grass
her black shoes shining
her stockings black
her skirt hem like a black bell
she clasps her black-gloved hands
and poses with a straight-lipped smile
the century she's born into
about to turn in two years though she's still
a child that day her hairline
capped in black
her hat like a two-tier mourning cake
boldly black, set sideways on her forehead
worn high as though balanced
as an exercise in posture and performance
adorned by two feathers
fanning above the brim, the quill
held in place by a broad black ribbon
her throat choked in white lace ruff
draping her breast like a bib
she seems amused to be alive
anonymous as stone

she's one of an octet
including her slightly older companion
a maid two years or so her elder
the bride, the mother of the bride
the groom

doomed to die within the span of two years
and two Chinese men
in oriental dress, their coat sleeves
fanning out twelve inches longer than their arms

all the men
sport facial hair
the Americans with beards
much like the Prince of Wales
the Chinese with trimmed moustache
though only one retaining the long braid of the Ming

but back to the girl
on the left
she is eleven or thereabouts

outside of the vantage of the frame
she will age
court and be courted, learn to love and be loved, wed
and be wedded, experience the sweet intimacies
of the marriage bed, then the agony of childbirth
motherhood, the long surmise of middle age, become
elderly, widowed, infirm, forgetful
fade away
— even
those who knew her
when they were young and
she was old have died and died again from memory
beyond recall

but on that day of her youth

first caught in the brief illumination of the lens
and then drawn forth
from the clarifying emulsion of the darkroom
the breath that shaped her dust
was full of the promise of a quickening heart gone slow

is not this ... (a Haibun)

... is not this a brand plucked out of the fire

Zechariah 3, ii

into the throng
one woman carries
the burdens of her faith

Ida Wight née Emerick had been a teacher in Canada. A product of the normal school education of her generation of young women, marriage would not have been an option for her since married women were not allowed to teach in Ontario in the late nineteenth century. Much like the brides of Christ, teaching was a profession of virgins, maids, celibate women, spinsters, schoolmarms and the mostly femme sole of the classroom. She taught for several years in the Ontario elementary school system before entering the missionary service in the United States and from thence she traveled to China where she ministered to the converted as a proselyte of her faith.

he came as light
into my faith
how deep it goes, this love
this moonlit water
of the mind

Ida married fellow missionary Charles Wight and gave birth to their first and only child. Their daughter was named Frances after Ida's German- American grandfather Francis Emerick.

nine months
I carried your name
hello my second heart

Shortly after Frances' birth the Boxers, so called because of their skill in martial arts, raged against the foreign presence in China. Calling themselves I Ho Ch'uan, or "the Righteous and Harmonious Fists," they despised Christian missionaries, and Ida was forced to flee for her life with her baby girl at her breast, but not before her young husband would succumb to pneumonia.

the moon alone
without the sun
all darkness unaccompanied

★

among the weeds
we wear the night

bereft

Ida would remain an unmarried widow for the remainder of her life and her daughter would know only one parent.

my child   alone
we walk the world

two lives engraved by ghosts on stone

★

I am
the lonesome daughter of an eidolon
a wife
of graves
the mother to a fatherless child

Shortly after having given birth, she is driven from her Chinese home. On threat of death she flees. A half-starved refugee, she walks almost a thousand miles in a river of human woe, surviving on soup made from water and shoe leather, carrying her yearling child in her arms, crossing China and then Korea on foot. Arriving at a port of exit, she takes a ship to America where she remains until the Boxer Rebellion fails and order is restored, making it safe to return to China. A missionary widow, her girl child in tow, she returns to the mission in the far east where she resumes her missionary role. She prospers there, first becoming a teacher and eventually serving as superintendent of missionary schools.

dying into the darkness
my life
of exhausted light

★

milk gone dry
like chalk on stone

the thirst in my daughter's mouth

★

whose God is this
allows
the louse to thrive

★

strike the rock
of faith
all hunger proves it stone

how loveless the sky

blue silence
beautiful and cruel

★

if I fall
into one dream

I plunge through darkness into death

★

if I sleep
in wakeful light

I see the sweet illusion
of an inner night

★

come home
the ocean wants

two shores

★

our lives
have fathoms beyond our reach
we are become

drowned swimmers of the breathless deep

★

When Shining Dreams

How like
the blind astronomer
my hands
in service of the light
unseen
go seeking in the darkness
for the stars
within the mind
the moon
where shining dreams

A Person on Business from Porlock

There is an imam
mosqued in the empire of the west
who preaches
that the greatest sin
in the land of the golden mountain
is the American lawn
even the burning earth
of south Texas, even there
on the torpid border of old Spain
that stolen-water-green thing thrives
with a great thickening
of wide-bladed
low-growth St. Augustine grass
even there
in the blue boil
of the unusable summer pools
of suburbia
in that necessary evaporate cool
all along the arroyos
the dry brown rivers
of parched clay
thirsty mud cracking open
like oil on old canvas
in the brilliant mirror of an unreflecting sky
the monolithic malady of modern paradise
insists itself
between the dream houses
of every middleclass mind

if one thinks of Cathay

and the Khan's palace
in the city of Chandu
where mare's milk spills
like moonlight on marble
and light falls in chords through cracks
like strands of silk that brace the bamboo palace
where leopards slip the saddle
in let-loose leaps
and the jessed hawks fly
over the claw shade of a shadow-measured wall

as I think now
of my own neighbour
mowing his yard for
the fourth time today

or as it was
with the woman next door
who plucked cut blades
one by one
from the sweet fragrance
of her wet-sock work with a similar care
one might use to pull stray thread
from a new garment

and I also recall
the mad lady nursing lost leaves
at midnight
in the candle-glow under star-dark heaven
when the world is otherwise laudanum black
and behind the forehead

like stones in a deep stream
something sleeps
turning green

She Performs

poem based on a glass plate photograph circa 1902

late in her life
the dowager empress Cixi poses and is
photographed
in the fragrance of apples
the air she breathes in the moment
sweet with the perfume of western fruit
she is seated
cross-legged, clothed
in a yellow floor-length gown
embroidered in paisley smocking
a purple imago at her breast
adorned in a spray of pearls
her feet concealed in beaded box-toed shoes
also fringed in river pearl
her hands
festooned in gilded fingernails
two long sharp decorative talons of wealth
worn on her third and fourth fingers
and she glances to the left
as though
catching sight of something
peripheral
something important concerning
the quintessential privacy of the soul
her small body
set in its crimson throne
like an actress in an opera—she performs ...
no longer the *dragon lady* of cliché

she becomes the mist
adrift in an orchard
the spirit
caressing the bone

and in years to come
the Republican army thieves
who desecrated her tomb
to plunder for jewels
who left her corpse exposed
feeling neither fear
nor reverence
for this once powerful woman

her disturbed remains
and the meaningless mausoleum
could not possibly have imagined this event

how we die into the past
whether by a thousand cuts

or by the one shallow snip
of indifference
like breath in dust

the glass plate fades in brilliant light
and the scent of apples dissipates
from the room
as if it were but a whispering of lost recall
or the locked-away darkness of dream
                          Reveal

the soul belongs
below the stairs, in the closet
in the crawl space
in the corn rows
in the bushes
in the wild wood
in the breath-stirred seed kites of glowing dust
in the tall weeds
in the sun-gold grain field
out of the flowering earth
out of the fertile swale
where the sweeter secrets
of living self-so
astonish the light
of the natural world
even on the dew-milkened grass
shining like green silk
even in the quiet enclosure of a white heart
like something come clear
in the burning fog
or the clarified darkness
of nightfall from gloaming
as it is with embers in ash
crimson with the memory of fire
or deep within the fragrant rose
that bends the stem
before it blooms
we are boundless
in the flesh-and-bone promises of time
we were all once first things new

though now
what thrills the frost
but warming
and the rattled wisdom
of a wintering oak
must wait to shade the graves of spring
like the cooling cloth of a fever room
where *nothing* draws us from delirium
into the blue mind of an empty sky
to the silence full of silence
like what the sleeper sees in sleep
between the veils of dream

Considering Ancient Chinese Erotica

in the spring palace
behind high walls
of the Forbidden City
the perfumed concubine
lolled with her bound-as-a-child body
lamed by beauty
the crimson water lily of the royal house
playing bring on the clouds and the rain
with the wealthy lords
of the Ming
in the court of songs
otherwise dishabille women
their misshapen bones
broken in slippers
crippled by pain her feet made small as a deer
for the visual delight of men
well-born girls
wearing bow shoes embroidered in silk
walking with the lotus gait
the short-step sway of pampered ladies
even in time the eldest daughter of the poor
wanting to marry highborn
achieved the crescent moon
of the cramped arch
with its erotic allure
an intimate and chaste concealment
lasting a thousand years
until the corseted Christians
came at the time of the heavenly foot
their own vital organs cramped

in whalebone
their tight breasts swaddled
in winding-cloth white wear
sending home souvenirs
amazing the congregation
amusing the minister
tantalizing all future museums
where horrified visitors troop past
in clicking stilettos and blushing tattoos

The Superintendent

looking at the comfortable room
in the luxurious home
she had built for herself
in the orient
my cousin said of our late aunt
posing like widowed gentry
lolling amongst her precious things
"I thought missionaries
 were supposed to be poor ..."
her silk pillows
embroideries
gilt upholsteries, silver
tea service, fine cloth
painted vase, and
exotic high-buttoned
tight-bodice dress, the tats
and flounces—doyen
of the wealthy classes
mistress of a private school
privy to the Sino-Victoriana
of a distant land that changed the mind
like the slow conversion of green
in slanting shade
where everything greys
in the lonesome lamentation of a solitary light

growing older
in a homeland no longer home
in the piano parlour silence
with that deep-toned quiet
of untouched ivory, each key
yellow as a smoker's tooth
who does not fear
or loathe to hear
the superintendent of schools
with her disapproving
and ultra-grammatical
crepitation, clearing her throat
with a phlegmy "ahem"
from the back of the room
her spine as stiff as a pointer
she strides
her heels cracking the floor
as she seizes the chalk of the day
and with white streak
screeching
is it a sin or is it a dream of sin
to see through the third eye
how the children tremble
shading their work
for a smudge of errors
the grand failures
we feel in the pedagogical squint
of the once-a-term stranger
in a classroom smelling of spilled ink
and the bass notes of old plasticine
fragrant in bent fingers

and multi-coloured snakes of clay
rolled flat on the modelling board
one name carved deep
in the cave of every desk
for we are the bullied, the shy
the wild, the plump
the brilliant, the lost
the bratty, the eager-to-please
the quiet, the pimpled
the unclean, the poor
the criminal, the crippled, the maimed
the doomed-to-die young
the bad seed, the sniffling, sniveling
easy-to-hate tattle tale
the pampered
the beaten, the bewildered
the too-stupid-for words
learning one lesson in a tall cone-shaped hat
under tousled hair

and one in the tasseled
mortarboard

we all share our nature with the dead
one name carved deep in the cave
of every empty desk is yours
and one name there is mine

At Least for Now

poem inspired by a photograph of Ida Wight in her home in China in the early 1930s

a lean woman
her long-boned body
draped in a black silk dress
she is seated
in a stiff-spined rocker
her well-shod feet crossed
at the ankles
adorned in high-top shoes
laced almost to the knee
like greaves
she grips the arms of the chair
as though at any moment she means to rise
or rather resist
the weightless phantom
that floats her spectral complexion
from the white collar
of this pale-fleshed visage
she, with the self-assured
physiognomy of the righteous
certain of the purity of her Christian soul
with the rectitude
of a widowed woman
bearing the carriage and posture of
her place in time

surrounded as she is by

the proof—her piano, her fern
her umbrella closed up and hung with its rainless verdict
and the cut-flowers
long-stemmed and blooming from a slender clear-glass
     vase

she is wasp-waisted
angular
doyen of a sun-bleached white-walled room
as on this day
she poses
in her parlour in China
and she means
to be herself forever

at least for now

Foreign Devil

before you came
to this much troubled land
where lives were lost
and lost and lost again
in ever-repeating waves of war
millions upon millions
dying under the black flag
the brilliant dragon banners
rising and falling
to the terrible wingbeat
of history

elsewhere your ancestors, the Irish
diaspora starved
in the blighted fields
the punk nightshade
oozing black to the thumb
like burnt grease cooled
elsewhere in the land of your first mission
America cried out
in chains
and the lash-lines of a coming storm
while in the heavenly kingdom
of the much hated Ching
where you would one day go
it was said

the people fear the officials;
the officials the foreign devils,
and the foreign devils fear the people

and the Taiping rose
and the Taiping fell
eleven years and the leader captured
and decapitated
though he was
committed to the natural foot
and enlightened reforms of a peasant state
the Manchu ascended
and the old dowager
took the throne of fear
a woman of cold-blooded ferocity
and homicidal rage
and it was she
residing in the pavilion
of the summer palace
presiding over affairs of the celestial empire
when you arrived
in that divided land
demarcated, carved into regions
and mapped into cut-away spheres of influence
and foreign powers
the Tsar, the English queen, the
Kaiser, the Emperor of Japan, and
also—the me-too Americans
you set your Christian heart
beating to the task
spreading the word of Christ
in land
soaked by blood
like sunset on the slaughtered edge of evening
when the blue day dies

with a crimson scream of a usurped sun
and the new night blackens heaven
blazing with uninvited stars

Snow

translation of a poem by Mao Tse Tung

This is a scene of the land to the north
Sealed in ice for a thousand li
A thousand miles of snow in force
From the great wall and beyond I see
Where the vast white windswept river makes
The Yangtze's frozen torrents still.
While mountains dance like silver snakes.
Great elephants of wax from hill to hill
Climb up the sunset crimsoned sky
To clothe the white dress with a red
Enchanting all where heroes vie
To win the landscape for their bed.
But emperors Shihuang and Han Wu Di

Uncultured men with lack of learning
And of Tang and Sung each dynasty
Had rulers crude and undiscerning.
And Genghis Khan of golden sky
Bent only his bow to the eagle's eye
In the glorious hunt of a time gone by.
To find kind heart and noble brow
We must look for them in the here and now.

Mao Tse Tung (1936) translated by John B. Lee

So the Story Goes

i

in my father's family
it seems
Mary was a doomed name
his sister
whom he loved, and who loved him
died by her own hand
in lonesome despair
she'd been a wild girl
who'd married badly
taken the apprentice butcher
given to drink and just no good
into her bed
come to wedlock
a ruined bride
then to be abandoned in the city
chasing his shadow
like a wind-blown weed
her twelvish daughter
rescued, brought home
to be raised on the farm
while Mary, her mother
erasing her name
from the book of life
was waked in the parlour
after the end of the war
the family
constructing a pretty lie
to mask the unacceptable sin of suicide

and I have
a photograph
of Mary as a child
her father and mother
gripping her chubby arms
all of them seated
in front of the scalding shed
the windmill strut
rising over my young grandmother's
left shoulder
the wind in the world like a ghost

and I wonder
are they raising her up
or holding her down
those three lives
caught in the past
her name a pencil scrawl
above those working hands
the land on the knuckles
the veins in the earth
the soil in the cloth
like clouds on stone
they hold their breath
and grin

ii

so
the story goes
Stella had set her cap at Herb
she the young schoolteacher
from the village
he the handsome shepherd
from the farm
skating tall and strong
stalwart on the ice of the flooded field
famous for miles
good loam in summer
rich land
black earth, fertile
for wet-foot corn
setting the hen's claw
of its root
deep in the glebe
but autumn brought water
and spring twin lakes
that seeped away slow
and winter the big freeze
and so
she came and caught him
knocked him flat
as a haymaker's desire
gave him nine children
four griefs and five joys

and Mary, her firstborn
the sorrow she cradled
the way it bothers
the breast
the hurt of a broken heart
like smothered burning
of a frost line heaving a stone
through buried smoke

iii

And Mary, Herb's sister
who died at twenty-one
of a virus of the mind
whom Ida had taught
in her class age eleven
an average girl
of ordinary gifts
except for her kindness
and her much-acknowledged
qualities of heart

her father
gone quick for the doctor
she passed
into a second more permanent sleep
while he lashed his horse
for home
too late
she'd weakened away
to whiteness in her bedclothes
like lime brushed gauze

what calms the dead
or cools the shaded glade
or makes the flesh fade
might make of life
a leafless branch bone-black on snow

and this
the ink that borrows breath

to make
the sorrow real

has loss to name
and name to lose

oh drop the tethered cup
within the well
and feel how full
the draw

iv

I have a photograph
of Mary Louisa Lee
a debutante
nineteen-year-old farmer's lass
two years to live

her hair
swept up in a straight part
her forehead
high and white
her eyebrow arched upon the right
her mouth a thin black line
the vermillion border
parenthetic to the shadow of her chin

you are dressed
in white flounce
full sleeves
ruffled like a bird
your face the common pale
of housework
of study away from the sun on the field

and then
there you are
caught in a second glance
the common Victorian photograph
of the dead
clothed in your black silk cerements
the ivory button

choked high and fastened at the throat

the morbid gaze
of a young woman
laid to rest at home

the dust on the glaze of the glass
and the milk of the eye
the same

Hussies Don't Wear Girdles, Girls

for Dorothy Lee Kay

Stella warned her daughters
"always wear your girdles
respectable and modest women
worry about the flesh
that jiggles"—
and "hussies don't wear girdles, girls"
she added—
still, her eldest daughter Mary married badly
a bride in trouble
at the altar, she gave birth
a few months short of nine months wed
after leaving the farm
and then the years unfolding sadly she
abandoned her twelve-year-old child
leaving her to fend for herself alone in an apartment
in the big city

Mary became the wild wife
chasing her man
a butcher's apprentice
a nogoodnik
hard drinker, bad seed
with an eye for the ladies
and he left her alone in the night
her spirit cracked
like hard clay in a dry wind until
she took her own life
and thereby entered

the long and soothing lie of family lore
for everyone said she died of a weak heart

and if we laugh to think of the foolish passions
of the past, or if we fail to feel
the bone-cold winters that sometimes come
to the soul of youth

we too might wish to gird the body
with a better darkness
and the mind with a warmer light

Now and Then

now
I know
that I've slept
in the bed that she died in
as I've waded
waist deep
in the green whisper
of tall grass
waving its seed in the sun
in the slow rye wind
of my lilac redolent youth
on my grandmother Woofenden's farm
vanishing into recall
under the shadow sweep
that darkened the beards
of the grain
like what happens
to faces with time
over summer
loud with cicadas in song
the katydids sawing their legs
itching their bodies for noise
with a shrill
stridulation of insect lust
in the cane berries' brightening light

and I know
that I've dreamed
in the knowledge of ghosts
in the nights

that have darkened the glass
and polished the glaze
like the blackness of ice
thin with cold

then and there
in my less strong youth
here and now
in my less strong age
is it what I remember
or what I imagine, I wonder
that carries the light of the moon
to that room

In the basement of the Mary Webb Centre
I handle your sent-home silks

in the basement
of the Mary Webb Centre
I handle
your sent-home silks
in what was once
the psalter-scented cellar
of your long-dead father's first church
where I learned
to name the many books of the Bible
in the smaller
glassed-in rooms
of Sunday-morning lessons
where I raced over
the painted cement floors
at Tyro
playing cosom hockey
with a sawed-off Koho
where I sat in a
small circle of village children
being a boy among peers
under the steady guidance
of the reverend Cross
who also came to our school
with stories of Christ
his pastoral face fading
from my mind
like the over-washed image
of old memory
where colour weakens in sunlight
to stain the paper it's soaked in

that same important building
where I sat
with Hope Palmer
sharing her strawberry box social
picnic basket
for the name I'd drawn for luck
her lunch redolent of dill sprigs
and the high pong of untinned salmon
a girl in white lace gloves, looking
as though her hands were dipped to the wrist in milk
and she sported fancy frilled socks
and Mary-Jane-bowtie-patent-leather shoes
a napkin in her lap
for catching the crumbs
as we moved through
the slow confusion of childhood
through youth
not yet blooming
in the contemplative silence
that comes in the awkward quiet
between the genders
brought together too soon
for reasons
they cannot comprehend

that room lost
under the upstairs pulpit and the spires
thrusting up and through the branches of maple
with a thousand-thousand funereal sundowns
draping the roof
in a dark web

with the eternal droning
of the window wells of winter
and the mostly shallow drifting
of shadow-blackened snow

and I am there
studying the oriental embroidery
of a small coat
and delicate slippers
like garments
from the costume chambers
of an actor's abandoned closet
someone famous
in the glory days of Gilbert & Sullivan
everything rain-stained
and threadbare
and tatterdemalion
like time-crushed roses
exhausting their fragrance
in the heart of a hundred closed pages

imagine morning
in the mulberry stain of dawn
after the silk moth harvest is done
with women at their handlooms
weaving
the headspring of beauty
singing Lei Su songs
for the wife of emperor Huang-ti
leaving their blue belief
in the soft fabric of fallen heaven

cut into sleeve shapes
for small-shouldered girls
to wear
playing dollhouse at the farm
those radiant costumes
crossing the ocean
arriving here as though coming home
sailing over moonlit waters
like the light of a golden gloaming
caressing the west coast of America

I feel in this ghost weight of a shining fabric
the drape
of wet smoke
the slow smoulder of fog over bones
and blossoms
of the turning-brown chrysanthemums
of autumn

The Rape of Nanking

i

on the banks
of the Qinhui river
in the city of Nanking

the bodies lie in fallen form
their corpses heaped as though it were
a time for harvesting the hogs

one soldier stands alone
among the slain
leaning on his shining sword

the slaughtered children
of the coldest heart
their hearts like stones in frost

a woman in a photograph
her dress above her waist
her womb defiled
by an upright cane
planted like a flagless staff
in the small hill
of her open thighs

her vulva
the fertile crescent
of a spade scar darkening the earth
how is it that we

come to this ...

that someone's much-loved son
become the rapist
in his uniform
writes home to say

dear mother—I am well
remember me to all

ii

the head of a single citizen
decapitated in the siege of the city
sits like a ripe gourd
set in the living crotch
of a leafless winter tree

the sword that did this work
still sharp, stropped keen
on a leather strap or
honed in cold blue fire on a sparking wheel

what was his last thought
I wonder
just before the world went black
as the spilled ink of the pupil going large

now this man
grafted like the dream fruit of war
sees with dead eyes
the dark river
and by the dying light
of a waning moon
how at the mercy of a warring man
the light might be in candle-drown
a breath of flame too deep to hold

iii

the competition involved
two officers
vying to prove
who might kill the more
in the shortest time
with a single Samurai sword
and so
they went quick to work
like expert butchers building silence
to quiet the bawling of an abattoir
or fish gutters
cleaning the silver school of a single catch
leaving the vermilion offal
in livid threads
snotting at a slippery floor

but the object here
was human dead
the prowess
of a sacred warrior code

oh—set your tired watch
and weep
sharp tears of sand
to shape mandalas on a windswept tile of time

the salt that sees the fire
burning white
sees there

the man who wins and shines
the cypher of his crimson list
still bleeding
in a bloodless book

the rust that rots all swords
sets sunlight clotted through a windless cloth
while glory eats through steel

iv *after Li Po*

once I sat alone on Baffin
at the base of Thor
that mile-high rock face
on the shore
of the Weasel—feeling there
all the wild energy of new water
and the great breath of the valley
roaring in the sun
how the universe might hold the mind
in its cold white basin
the luminous blue
striations of millennial ice
crushed into strata
by time's ten-thousand winters
that are barren and lifeless
and there and then
in that lonesome moment
at that isolated place
in the long shadow of that natural monument
in the idle stillness
of my smallest solitude
I caught in the rills of melt
and the runnels of an overflow
going full to the frozen sea
how the light might thirst
for the purity
of well-wine drawn
from the dropped-deep cup of the absent self

v   *after Basho*

we passed along the razorback
and from there
walked into the clearing
of the abandoned Lake Erie estate
where deer
were grazing in the meadow
under eagle-gaze
and wild turkey
loud in their black flock
fed nearby

and I sat
and took in their number
as a hen might
count her poult
by jake and by jenny
in the feather-measure of mid-day

meanwhile in the frog temple of the swale
the pulsing black jam jar
of parenthetic spring
turned green
with new-featured spoor
what is the available ovarity
of the ovum-fertile moon
cross-threaded by frog father
of dapple-variant day

by Basho's grace

and Li Po's light
and by the cold shop
of these same unseen stars

this sun we share
this moon we hold within
as common as a coin
passed palm to palm

this song, the one we sing
the one we hear
in days not long enough
for thoughts unending night

vi

if I face the shadow
then it turns away

if I run
the shadow leads or follows
as it marks the path
with footsteps little seen

if I am still
and close my eyes
to set the shadow free

I then become the shadow
larger then for all the things
I only seem to see

Via Dolorosa
>   *from a Photograph Taken on Bloody Saturday*
>   *During the Battle of Shanghai*

what might we make of the value of life
if we live
in a place
at a time
when the truths that we cherish

   won't hold

for even the proof of the soul of a child goes
lost like the beauty of snow
caressing the dark swell
of an unseen
and unseeable sea
in the far off lonesome vastness
of a blackwater night
starless with stars
and moonless with moon

somewhere elsewhere than this
surely two lovers lie
in sweet involvement
their heartbeats greeting through bone
each mind
like a hand with its palm to the pane
of the house of the world
lighting a lamp where it glows in the flesh
and pleasure

transforms as it fades
like the smoke of a withering wish

how conceiving completes
with its chain of edulcorate verbs
the meaning and mystery
of darkness made good
and of faith going deep

all adoration and delight
alive in the liquefied locus
of heaven's grand milken of life

then what of the child
burned in the war
the baby alone on the earth
and orphaned by fire
who screams on the tracks near Shanghai
and is famously photographed in forgotten
suffering of history which is always
quiet on the page
and silent in the text held closed

so forgive this ink if it requires the
lifting of anguish made loud
so agony sobs with your voice
and misery wails in your unquiet ear
in language that scorches the tongue like a fire-sharpened stick

Black Christmas

Christmas Day 1941
Black Christmas
the day Hong Kong surrendered
suffering under Japanese occupation
January the fourth 1942
a notice appeared
in an English-language newspaper— all enemy nationals
to assemble on Murray Parade Grounds
though many failed to see the notice
1,000 gathered on the grounds
in addition to those who congregated voluntarily
others were forcibly removed from their homes
the assembled were marched to
and initially interned in hotel-brothels
on the waterfront near Macau Ferry Pier

conditions were dirty and overcrowded
the food poor
after 17 days
the internees were removed by boat to Stanley

enemy nationals who failed to assemble
on Murray Parade Grounds
avoided internment at the hotel-brothels
by January's end
most civilians were moved to Stanley

upon arrival at camp
internees discovered little preparation
no cooking facilities no furniture
scarce crockery little or no cutlery
toilet facilities were filthy inadequate waterless stinking pestilent
rooms overcrowded with random assortments of internees
unrelated to each other
and with little attention paid to hygiene or public health
thus they would live
thus they would die
by execution
from disease

food provided by the Japanese authorities
contained dust mud rat excreta
cockroach excreta   cigarette butts
and sometimes dead rats
every morning internees were served rice congee
at 11 a.m. and 5 p.m
meals consisting of rice with stew

the teachers and educational administrators
amongst the internees
provided lessons for the children

one-hundred-and-twenty-one internees
perished in the camp
two died from falls
one child drowned
on 16 January 1945
an American plane accidentally bombed

Bungalow 5 at St. Stephen's College killing fourteen
seven internees were executed
having been in possession of a radio
internees were forced to witness their torture after which
the internees were shot
aside from this
the Japanese authorities had executed by decapitation
three Chinese policemen
for bringing cigarettes and tobacco into the camp
on September 23rd 1943
Ida Wight, one of seventy
repatriated Canadians
on board the ship
Teia Maru
departed for Goa
in an exchange of prisoners
and so entered the final phase
of a life
caught up in the faux Chinese
curse "may you live in interesting times"

Thus the Wild Fox

"thus the Wild Fox was introduced to the very highest circle
and the throne"

I have stood like a tourist before
the empyreal throne of China
at the threshold of the inner sanctum
of the heavenly palace of the Forbidden City
and seen there
the inspiring vacancy
of empty furniture
and how time
and circumstance conspire
against majesty
making vacuous presence settle into
the seat of an ordinary chair
from darkness brought low to the floor
like the swollen shadow of fat fruit

and the dowager Empress Cixi
no longer there
and the Wild Fox
who plotted her assassination
gone, and all of Europe
the Tsar, the Kaiser
Victoria, Archduke Ferdinand
Emile Loubet, and in the
orient Meiji of Japan
all involvement with intrigue
secrets and lies and rumours of war
in the wars of the world

in Korea, in Vietnam
in Crimea, South Africa
Cuba—empires ripening
in Sudan, Palestine
on the borders of burning maps
everywhere the dead branch sways
over the changeable coasts of the earth-cutting sea
and if we fail, then
to genuflect or
quake
on the verge of evidence
concerning
how things once were
such is the way in museums
of dishonest memory and fantastical dream
and so it is as with the wind of dying
the ephemeral storm remembers the tree
in shapes of breaking
when darkness shrinks from falling
and silence rattles the eternal absence of a winter leaf

Our Own Particular Time

she was living
in the thrall
of big themes
within the great wide and life-sweeping
storms of war
every enthusiastic ideological
ideal—an inferno, a conflagration
scorching its way over landscapes
and seascapes
like the warp and woof
of the weave of a great and horrifying
tapestry of flame
or like the shaken fist
of town leveling rain
leaving the ugly smothering
mud-deepening flood
of dark thought in its wake
this way came fascism
its black sleeve
shadowed by the mad ulna
of tyrannical hate
misanthropic blood and soil
and the rot of the soul
that way
the shibboleth of angry weather
blood on the flag in a circle of sun
the divine wind
raping the coast of the world
a smoulder on the map of the mind
like the crawling of fire through grass

meanwhile in the mountains of Mao
the swarming locus
of another anti-empirical plague
and from the west
the liberating drone
of a golden-voiced huzza
those death bringers
with a fungal cloud of German science
and a screaming wind

what of Marxism
what of communism
what of fascism
what of despotism
what of these
might a human make
give the camp guard his due
give the policeman his due
give the soldier his due
give the patriot his due

we are all here
on the prayer wheel
of our own particular time

turn your palm to the sun
see there
the silken privilege
of a soft hour

five moons to the floor

and the heart

in its cave of ice

Send Me the Names

she lived at the last
in Durban by the sea
she dwelt in rooms of privilege
thick in swarms of change
and though she thought herself in paradise
she also saw the suffering
and ruined earth
the awful denouement of nations
shaped by map's ephemeral surmise
black orchids and the dragon's jaw
the golden morning
and the crimson hiss of night
her future now
in volumes of the past
with old Hiroshima blooming and reborn
as something
rising from the rubble
still in flame
and lines demarking cities
of the mind
too high to climb

Apartheid where she lives
and war in Seoul about to start
she sent
a postcard to the farm
addressing issues
like a songbird chirming
on the cusp of coming storm
tell me of the boys from home

send me the names
among the Execroi—
the volunteers—

she said she longed to climb the fence
to fetch the milk—
or drift like weather
on a carpet bound for Canada
again—

and as she wrote
those lines

the globe in shadow
changed its mask of shades

and nations faded in and out
as though from blackened whites
of cloud-crossed snow

and though true ink
might grip a moment
as it dries

it also blots its counter page
with unintended lies

The Importance

Every fourth Sunday at communion
robed in red service with white surplus angel sleeved
fanning open at the lifting of my arms

I shared sweet dregs drawn forth
from darkness
left welling in the chalice
as an overpouring by our village
priest who loved the drink

and I tasted the brassy flavour of the rim
tainting the flow
with its burning of fermented grape
as it wet the vermillion border of my lip
and warmed my tongue my gullet and my gut
to blush my callow flesh
a gulp for him a sip for me a gulp for him a sip for me
a final sip to stagger by
enough to send me slightly tipsy
tilting for the bishop's oaken chair
where I sat aslant
a giddy lad
a little giggle thinker
only ten years old

and there I mused upon
the metaphor of sacrament

this is my blood that was shed for you

how those essential words
rang out as long and deep as valley bells
that knell in waves
with painful wounds of sound
within my foggy-minded youth
as slightly drunk on wine and faith

I wondered at the cruelty of God

Because She Failed to Attend Her Sister's Anniversary

mayflies of this morning
caught in a weft of web
a sticky scrimshaw of tatterdemalion grey
etched on the ultra-white fascia
of a lakeside house

> *she remains forever unforgiven*
> *though she sends greetings home*
> *from the far harbour, ensconced as she was*
> *on the west coast*
> *of California*
> *wishing the couple well*

all things that fail to vanish
the grief and grievance of the living spirit
that leave their tracery
in a wind-swept whisper of flightless wings
the gauzy fray of ephemeral things

> *and years since then*
> *with the entire gathering*
> *gone to ghost*

a palm print
smudging the clarity of glass
marked by the moist lifeline of a child's hand

the delicate bone-work
of ice-veiled water
frost-gloved flowers

translucent moon valleys
milky cold and luminous
satellite with the feckless embrasure
of the soul within stone

    we are become
     the broken-hearted statuary
     of some future contemplation

where for the want of the silver mask
of the solitary self
all that remains of the mirror's eye
is the breathless breath of the mind   alone

The Blue and Boundless Cage of Paradise

on the first day
of the second half
of an old century
you chose to enter
the great mystery
held within the common clay
of almost all octogenarians
suffering the final quiet
of a stone-still heart

the obituarist took up his local pen
marking the time, as though
setting the hour of an open-faced clock
forever fixed by the tranquil departure
of one soul

the labour to silence of your lost breath
in the early summer
just before the falling of the great darkness of Apartheid
on your chosen land
with ocean combers
rolling ceaselessly rolling on the Durban coast
of that distant continent
you joined
into the enormous discontinuity of ordinary death
while here at home
in a cold world
awhirl with snow
the slow news came
and brought with it

the stale sorrow of familial loss

and in the moment past measure
as the feckless hand
drifts and sinks away
through last linens
like the pulsing ash of leaf blown shadow
fading with a lessening of light

I find my own beginning there
as I was first conceived
in winter, born in late autumn
in a month of cool rain and come-early darkness
that selfsame year

our paths
like grease on silk

the sky
the water wishes it were
in flight towards

the blue
and boundless cage of paradise

counting cranes ...

Mu—Not—lament for the lost kingdom of I am

the lion gate
on my desk lies open
on the left—the leonine child
on the right—the world
and in the centre
my name
in pictogram and inkpot
I am at the invisible gate
of the forbidden city of Mu

I have set these jade creatures
on coasters bracelet brown with coffee stains
from the Silk Road
of Marco Polo
and I am born in the year of the rabbit
and testing the dragon of my luck—for it is March
the equinox a half-a-week away
on the Sunday of Purim
from the story of the book of Ester
celebrating the liberation from Persia
tomorrow St. Patrick will drive the snakes from Ireland
with a green thought

during the long weeks of Lent
in the sign of Pisces
coming into spring with its sad Friday
and the cruelty of the Roman cross

I heard today
a hopeless soldier
falling to his knees
in prayer at Anzio in Italy a ghost of battle
importuning "help me God, help me Father
do not send your son—
this is no place for children ..."
and I am wondering
as I read a poem on the inner wisdom of objects

long after the mind gather
of this
solitary and most
singular incarnation

what anyone but I
will make of the meaning
of the bric-a-bracs on my windowsill
the stones and shell fragments
a vial of sand from Wadi Rum and beach glass
from Cuba and Korea and Thailand
—oh, the photographs, the sculptures
and flags of nation
will be easy to get wrong—

but the bricolage of strangers to my soul
I challenge with sunlight
pouring in like apple wine
that cruel to snow shadow line
marbling the ice with its grey patina
of chill moisture

like the wet windows of a cold frame
warming the seed bosom of frozen earth

and under the dormant russet
lies a ladder
fallen in the white froth of a filthy world
two feet in the air like a dead beast
a swollen step only the low fruit need fear
the lazy gather of lost gravity
equalized by the cruel energy of over-ripening
in winter's last hurrah

if the pencil maker
the paper maker and the poem maker
if only they could meet and share
one breath on the blank page and there
see everything I mean and everything I meant
my hand still moving and my hand is moving still
toward the light no longer there

A dream I dream on my first night in Beijing

in a dream of my grandson
he is riding
the mask of comedy over the blue lake
a three-week-old infant
clinging to a gilded grin
little Euripides
the butterfly imago
shaking his spear
at the water

and I am standing on the shore
watching him drift
and glide and rise
and fall on the thermals
the old tragedian
unworried and laughing like summer
in the philosophical sunlight
of golden creation

and he
a small god
pale hero of moonlight
and morning

if I wake I know
he will remain in motion
until I sleep again

Is Beijing burning

we walk the smouldering streets
and cross
the smoky square
amazed to see
the ashy patina
that clings
to smudgy paint-shine
on the cars
the sun unseen within an amber sky
an artificial overcast
chokes all the light
our stars like fire hissing in an almost
combustible fog
the moment we burn
the edge of memory away
to find
the lie we'll tell
to children in their chairs
the future is a fuel to storms
today Chicago's blackened sky
today the water wall
that drowns a dozen islands
in a leveling aftermath
high winds that break the heart
and snap the bones to candle-crush

and there above Tiananmen
outside the lion-guarded gate
the face of Mao Tse Tung
smiling down through blurs of smog

what's truth to him
or truth to us
or truth to anyone
dishonest ghosts
with much to say
tell stories from the grave

A boy speaks of his childhood in the countryside outside of Beijing

as a boy in China
he speaks of how
he dripped liquefied wax
upon the wings
of a cricket as with
the weeping of that warm seal
he changed
the pitch and timbre of the wee creature's
song
oh sweet harmonious
singing of a single voice
like Emperor Zhu Di
who out of loneliness
carried for company
the insect in its cage
throughout his isolated court
the shrill-voiced insect
his only friend ...

as I recall
from childhood
how they sang among towels
chirping through ablutions
their small black exoskeletons
like warriors in armor
the sharp ideal
of their high-pitched music
falling quiet
as I came closer

to discovery—in mutual wonder
we two leapt
he like the black notation
of a shrieked vowel
seeking the corner cracks
of the room
I   like a kettledrum
booming for the open door

Undeserving blue

the one-armed legless man
his flesh tattooed by fire
lay like
a statue broken in the street by war
set there
for charity
beside his cup of coin

and then
along the tourist route
a second man
folded in and crumpled
at the chest
his body withered up
like winter fruit
a single head for sadness
emerging from the rot
as though he swam
and took his breath
above the grey confusion of half-set concrete

their handlers
bring them here
each morning
set out for shop and trade
jade lions
at the palace gates
below the smiling face
of Chairman Mao Tse Tung
at night

the guilty commerce
shakes a shattered hand
to count the take

and in the darkness
at the end of day

we turn a wheel of stars
to find ourselves
within the memory of God
our fate
defined by seeming grace, perhaps
or something less than true
in what comes clear to us
tomorrow as we wake
in undeserving blue

Tea flower falling

I touch
one fragrant tea flower
then watch it fall away
in sweet descent, to trace
the trail of its perfume
through aromatic wisps of pinkish light
unpetalling the air
with sweeps of delicate drift
undressing distance as it goes
tumbling down among autumnal greens
its sister seeds
remain to fix their season
in a winter stone
these hillsides wait for spring
to feel the pluck and hold releasing the grip
of the picker's inch of leaf
to find the palm-dried flavour
of an expert hand
the ancient skill
elixir of the learned response
how then to shade this language
with a faded word, one moment brewed
within the mind, a supple monument
that energy of joy and breath suspended
in the melt
come now home's common frost
to mother water from my weeping thumb
the window smears the scene
revealing all within the heart-warmed eye
we sometimes do our better looking with

to love the world half seen
beyond the self
too much to be enough
an all-sufficient glance of grace
when ice that's clarified by rain
becomes the rain come clear

Climbing the Great Wall of China

I climb the stairs
to where the Great Wall
breaks its spine
along the grey-green ridge
of smoke and fog above the Yanshan Mountains
and as I rise
I carry nothing more
than a shadow's weight of daily cares
and as I glance
I am amazed to see
how worn away by walking
are the stones
beneath my feet
how smoothed as though
by water over time
and leather trod
eroded by the come and go
of hordes of trekking solitudes
and as I touch
a single shape of chiseled rock
I feel the slave's fardel
the spirit burden of a broken life
the fragment of an empirical fear
the horse's heavy heartbeat
on the warring earth
the blackened hoof
that thunders on the steppe
with arrows singing
in a mind of troubled dreams
I pause

to let a lucky tourist
take a photograph
his friend
leans smiling as she breathes
to catch her breath
her bosom heaves *alive alive* and lets it go

I'm warm enough to wait a while
my quickened pulse
is like my father
at my morning door
it knocks to wake
an answer from my over-weary bones

and if he's there, or not
I rise
and seek the purchase
of a greater height than this

Counting cranes

at high noon
standing on the Bund
looking east across Huangpu River
at Pudong skyline
cast in grey smoke
as though seen through
the ripening lens of an ageing eye
I think of the language of morning
when I talked over breakfast
with an American steel man
living here in Shanghai
since twenty years ago
in 1995 he said
half of the construction cranes
on the planet
were working in one city
meaning this new city
near the mouth of the Yangtze
in the financial district
all that I'd seen
the night before
illuminated and lovely
in the backdrop of an oriental night
dark and cast-iron black
holding Li Po's moon
like a sentry lantern
lit till dawn amazed by sleep
lost every artifice of light
and I remember
looking west and east

and east again
into that tall brilliance
dwarfing even the ziggurat
of ancient story in the rising voices of a broken world
when suddenly
a drifting scow
blackened our view
and like a knife in silk
the mind tore darkness to a plimsol line
from stem to stern
the ugly prow cut water so we rolled
upon its roiling wake
the shining city drowned in shimmering foam

if I say I prefer
the architecture
on the Bund
old Europe and her earth-brown brick
the commerce of a different age
less glassy in the gloss of time
the spread-wing gargoyle in the eaves
in flight through opium smoke
at the end of an era of war on war

what might the twenty-four million say

I've been to the Yu Garden
to the squat pagodas
and the natural stone sculptures
of a slower hour
and if my inbreath burns

like a dragon from the west
my outbreath also smoulders
at the river's bend building this poem
one scorched word at a time

The empty boat

when I see
the moon
over China

I cannot help
but recall

the lost life of Li Po

the drunken poet
drowning in a pond

the empty boat
a vacant afterthought
made more
buoyant by the absence
of the thinker
at the oars

how lonesome the light
without us

how dark
those brilliant beams

The Chinese on the moon

the news arrives today
informing this world
that the Chinese
have managed
to place a robot on the moon
sent out
into the myth of night
upon a fire ship
where science sets
its ineluctable eye
the powerful instrument
of the human mind
gone digging
through the frost-white rock
seeking sub-lunar soil
in deeper veins of unimportant dust
to find a thought of gold
the El Dorado
of the dark
empirical proof
of madness in the tides

from the menstrual crimson
of an oriental dawn
we take a breath of smoke
while glowing embers
of a burning star blink out

and blinded
by forgetfulness
forget again

I thought I was in China
held against my will

she says she did not fall
but rather
that she fainted, withering onto the floor

an old lady three days
slumped in clothing
like the nuisance of laundry to do

seventy-two long hours spent alone
in artificial darkness
lonesome for the light

and when she awoke

she said of her time
away

"… I thought I was in China
held against my will …"

her apartment floor in Paris
transformed to a locked cell in a distant land

her body
transported as though

truth in the mind
were the same as truth in the world

Suseok — viewing stones

my son, my grandson and I
were walking
the gravelly shores
of the Yellow Sea
on Daebu Island
looking west through amber sky
west to the entirely imaginary far-away
coast of mainland China
the sun
shining like a dulled brass gong
hung in soundless heaven
over the low-tide mudflats of Korea
and we were
looking to gather up
the most interesting stones
and only recently empty shells
the small cochlear conches
that hold the ocean winds of the world
as poems might hold
a meaningful breath
at the moment of deep-breath knowing

and I have gathered
my own little tea bowl
of chalk and silvery anthracite
carrying home the light of hope
brought here from these broken mountains
and that scaling off of iron oxide
from the water-loud coves
with their coming in and going away
of moon-drawn amplitudes

that swallow the road and drown the ankles
where the beach turns to vanish under
the afternoon drop-shadows
of the great engines of the sea
and as I hold council here
with silent beauty of granite
and pink rock
cobbled with dead creatures
who cling, barnacled
to the underbelly of a time-crushed
stratum and substratum
of cold vermillion

I think back
to the finding
when our three shades crossed
like the slow dampness of dragged black cloth

and there is this consolation to loss
the way memory
brightens
the shades and hues of meaning
like wave wash on dry rock
and tomorrow's freeze
that set the coast
in hard-white unwalkable shards of dropped ice

what we'd seen
beneath the heavy burden of winter
unpacking its load
on the threshold of a second morning

made everything
unavailable to the hands

but there
the heart reached through

An incident at the bridge of no return

in an assignment
involving a clear view
the young lieutenant
was trimming a particular poplar tree
so the Americans
might observe without obstruction
the deployment and movement
of enemy guns, and
training his axe
on the aspen with its shivering leaf
looking north
to the bridge of no return
he fell
from a fatal blow to the brain
from behind
the cold tool
blunting his last thought
like the dark wedge
where the burnt Y
of the barkless trunk
remains with its blackened knot
like a blind eye fastened at the fork
of two branches
it stands there
a scorched post crowned in rot
with us living on
in such
a ridiculous world
in the sad significance of risible things
where what matters most

seems valued least
and what matters least
is conserved
in the chiseled knowing of stone

The outset

at the foot of Gwanaksan mountain
at the outset of a wide trail
leading to the crags
and narrows above Seoul
where millions of city dwellers
take treks in the heart of the day
the sculptor Mr. Kim
has built a small house
at the gateway to beauty
and he sees us
stopping close by
admiring the poems
bannering the fence
in what to us is an unintelligible Korean script
and he emerges
comes to us, stalwart legged
a small sexagenarian man, smiling
strong in his bones
and he greets us
in a language we do not speak
grips us, with brilliant eyes
invites us in
to savour a morning coffee
black and sweet, fragrant
with the mildura of the burnt cane
of our common field

outside the door
a thousand hand-sized
Taegeukgi flags fly their four colours
in a winter breath
the red and blue
circumference a lovely circle
for uncomparing strangers
sharing the morning

he shows us
his own poem
a short piece on coming of spring
and the breaking of bread
by the chill
unfreezing of a snow-whitened stream

Timmy's down the well

as I am conscious
of the perils
of living in a world
that is bellum
and full with the falsity
of the fierce and terrible yawp of war
I send out
the kinder dog
of my most beautiful thought
and I am
wagging memory at important windows
I am barking
at the scriptoriums
of mad leaders
where oak drawers slide shut
on the keepsakes of life
I am howling
at the Lupercalia of a romantic moon
where light
and the mirror of light
are drawing in the muddy skirts
of my hometown waters
while the deeper ambitions of love
arrive and leave in waves
like the bridal bed
evenings and mornings
of warmed dreamers
who wake and sleep
in the swan tuck of angels

my son
who works and thrives
in government regions of Seoul
tells me
his school is at the epicenter
of the animosity of big guns
training their dark zeroes
at the soul of the city
and I know—
any sunrise
has its own Gallipoli
all moonsets in yellow air
might break shining glass
with a seismic whump of a great shattering
where we are all bad hammers
we are all
the pelt and pummel
of red stone and sharp sticks
on soft flesh

Mr. President
you with the burning tongue
take your crimson axe away
from my broken brain
I am here
singing from the common tree
among the magpies
among the crows
I come
palm line open to the blue ceiling
give the greater graves

the balm of a short shadow
I cast my longer darkness
onto the green recline
of an out-of-reach light
where we both breathe
we all breathe

and into this lasting language
of even the most ancient poets
I say, let Caesar weep
on the senate step
let him weep at the river
I refuse
the map lines of his desire
I bark
at the buoyant well holes
of my body
and am dangerous with a different
and far more powerfully resonant echolalia
of the resounding voice of a father's love

Broken time traveller

lying in the malodor of the midnight city
with our window open
to the burnt-black fragrance
of industrial winter
under a sky's starless ambient neon
of the urban neighbourhood of Gunpo
with factory smoke
drifting in from the fiery diseases
of commerce and labour
infecting the dream sickness
of this otherwise comfortable room
we are long married
and living
through the jetlag insomnia of broken time
we tumble together like river logs
in the cold inertia
of this new night
enduring the ennui of the deep-bone need
for sleep
at odds with the clock
and the grey gloom of a false hour

what asking there is, is
of the body
with its weird fatigue
the heart stumbles like a kicked drum
with its weakened want
to be doing
and doing again
that slow chore of its dutiful visits

at the pulse points
desire tapping its code
on the counterpane

if we are both awake too long
in the feckless melatonin
of an oriental dark
we are also becoming unwilling experts
of the bloom-light of dawn
the way it rises in the mind
like a waterline
the way it warms the glass
like wet ice
the way it suffers into the flesh
like the suffusing of a low-grade fever

saying to all the interfering exigencies
of sun-born day

get up, rise up
take up your bed and walk
into the great elsewhere
what waits is waiting
afterwards
there will be nothing to do
but this

The insatiable hungers of the sun

my five-year-old grandson
is racing along
the low perils of a park wall
flapping his arms against gravity
like the wingbeat
of a flightless bird
and there on the parapet he feels
in this the common thrill of childhood
that is almost always
cruel with grandfather fearing
the knockout
and the shin bark
the scab and scar of it
the memory of bone break
something splintered
something cracked
something snapped at the green graft
that hurts in the cold

and yet
he scatters over the cinderblock ledge
blinking safely past the accidental blinding
of a bare-branched hedge
on and through
the white stumble of each snow trap
rising and running
over the dead groan
where winter heaps itself into a rubble of shattered ice

and he stops

at the high point
where he finally leaps
and lands
and climbs again
being the daredevil of this sure-foot carousel

until he's brought in close
by the clutch and giggle
of two schoolgirls
who fancy his big eyes
and the handsome dash
of all that male energy
wanting its name
they embrace him, lift him like a big doll
set him in motion
run and chase and are chased by
the big blue-bellied shadows of the sun on the snow

last night we were speaking of spiders

and how
they weave their webs
from the outside in
and I have seen them
drifting on silk
from tree branches
from windmill struts
from window sills
dropping down and fearless
like steel workers
lashed to high scaffold
swinging out
and seeking a second hold
a third, a fourth, a fifth sticky fastness
going clockwise in the sun
and catching the light
in silver strands
with beads of dew for the roses
the glass in my study view
is ghosted grey
like a handprint
after the hand has warmed the glaze
leaving like breath
that intricate silver lifeline
of the quick eight-legged lady

in Mongolia
there are fossils
ancestored in stone
from a million years
of continuous spider life
etched like burn shadows
formed by threads and buttons
from the garments
of lost children
however, after I wipe clean
all midnight evidence
or skein my broom
in the sticky whirl
sweeping the soffits and rafters
the morning comes
and she wafts against darkness
wins the cross weave
tattered with mayfly wings
and delicate filaments of brilliant dust
where things would rather shine
and be bothered by blur
frail monuments
that want my attention for the fuller silence

Going back to the world

my second son
finds himself floating
on the muddy mirror
of the Mekong
riding the big blue lung
of a foreign sky
in the remote regions
of Thailand
old Siam having her say
in the sultry voice
of a hot river stillness
when someone upsets
the boat
and he spills
laughing into the coffee-brown
shallows that gulp
around his body
like the pull on the line
of a smooth-bellied catfish
thrashing on a soft hook of bent light

and he uses that occasion
to dive down
to plunge his hand
into the clam-grip of the muddy bed
retrieving one wet stone
for his father
who wants only this thing

however unglamorous

however ugly
he wants
a river rock
or scree from a ruined hill
something a hen might swallow
to grind poor grain

a dull enough thing
not to be missed
by the mountain
nor mourned by the delta
nor grieved by the field

a dull enough thing
like at home on the lake
the glacial child of a big grinder
melting backwards
from the ten-thousand-year-old dawn
of an ancient
and even more primordial day than this

the fanned out energy
of a big crush
embossed on its facets
and bent at its curves

let diamonds and gold and silver
moil themselves
in the worm-heart of history
kings in their coffers
and other velvet-robed

panjandrums of the temple
the glint in the eye of a greedy council

his father
wants only
the privately precious dross
something marked by the local light
and culled
for lack of beauty but for this:
it was there
in the footstep darkness
of an all-ancestoring night
when empire rose and fell
to the silk breath of a dying counterpane
with maidens gathered in dew

my son knows
his father to be
just the sort of simple man
who like everyone
with a palm line
open to the alms of dawn
might wonder
at want and worth

Ida Wight (a biography)

My father George Emerick Lee's middle name means leader. It can be traced by way of his grandmother Mara Crosby's maiden name back through three generations to her grandfather Francis (Frank) Emerick, a German-American emigrant from New York State, who arrived in Haldimand County, Upper Canada as a young late-come loyalist in search of cheap land circa 1805.

Though he never seems to have gone by the name Franz, it is possible that English was his second language. His own father almost certainly would have spoken German at home. Frank settled briefly on a small parcel of land near the Haldimand tract bisected by the demarcation line for south and north Cayuga. There he spent a few years clearing the property prior to being caught up in the War of 1812. Pressed into service as a private in the Lincoln militia, he fought at both the Battle of Ogdensburg and the Battle of Crysler's farm. After being released from duty in 1819, he came home with his health compromised by winter warfare. Shortly after his return he saw fit to make application for land in the London District claiming that his health was poor and that his landholdings had been diminished by expropriation relating to Native Land claims along the Grand River. He resettled near what is now the ghost town Napier. There he prospered as a farmer, raised a family, and is buried along with his wife in an abandoned churchyard.

Emerick is of Roman origin, though subsequent to that, it is a name that can be traced to the Rhine region of Germany. As it is with many Germanic American names in Upper Canada it is associated with the Loyalist diaspora fleeing persecution in post-revolutionary United States.

The primary character in my story is Frank's granddaughter, my great-aunt Ida Wight (nee Emerick). Following a brief career as an elementary schoolteacher, she joined the China Inland Mission. Shortly thereafter she arrived in China as a young missionary, met and married a fellow missionary named Calvin Wight, and gave birth to their only child, Frances. Within a year she found herself widowed and in distress during the tumultuous Boxer Rebellion. Although it is not certain, it seems likely that her young husband fell victim to the rabidly xenophobic Boxers who were especially violent toward white foreigners in general and missionaries in particular.

Ida fled China on foot, carrying her baby daughter Frances in her arms. She and Frances survived by drinking broth made from shoe leather and boiled cotton. Two years later, after the rebellion failed and order was restored, Ida returned to China where eventually she served as a superintendent of schools. Living in relative comfort for nearly forty years, she luxuriated in a privileged and prosperous life until the Japanese invasion in the late 30's followed by the bombing of Pearl Harbour in December 1941. Shortly after that she was placed in Stanley internment camp in Hong Kong. Her daughter and her grandchildren were interned as well. Liberated by the Americans, she departed for Durban, South Africa where she remained until her death.

This book deals with three generations of my ancestors living in Canada. My great-great grandfather Francis Emerick, born in 1790 sired seven children. The seventh of these was my great-grandfather John Emerick, a Methodist minister who died tragically young leaving a widow and two fatherless daughters. He perished from sepsis, an infection that set in due to an injury suffered at a logging bee. His second daughter Ida, the aforementioned protagonist of this book, died on the first day of January, 1951, eleven months before I was born. Mara, her elder sister and my great-grandmother married a hardware merchant named Crosby. Their daughter Stella Crosby married my grandfather Herbert

Mercer Lee. George Emerick Lee, my father was their youngest child. Like my father, I came to possess a middle name taken from the matrilineal line.

Notes on the poems

The Impossible Black Tulip: inspired by the fact that many of the early Chinese emperors were inclined to believe that the world beyond the borders of China was so mysterious, unknowable and insignificant as to be impossible to map

Celestial China: inspired by the fact that the earliest recordings of the night sky were made by Chinese astronomers who documented sightings of Haley's Comet recorded on a sky map called 'The Silk Atlas'

A Person on Business from Porlock: the title of this poem is an allusion to the stranger who came knocking at Samuel Taylor Coleridge's door thereby interrupting the composition of his laudanum dream poem "Kublai Khan"

So the Story Goes: When Ida Emerick taught school in the village one of her students was my great-aunt once removed Mary Lee. Mary's report card reveals her to have been a rather poor student. She died on the farm in her twenty-first year and was waked there in the parlour

Hussies Don't Wear Girdles, Girls: is a comic interlude taking its title from Ida's niece Stella Lee née Crosby's (my paternal grandmother daughter to Ida's sister) advice to her daughters concerning female decorum as to manner of dress

In the Basement of the Mary Webb Centre: in the village where Ida taught school there is an art centre that was originally a United Church. Ida's father was a minister there. On one occasion when

I was doing a reading at the centre the host had kindly brought Ida Wight's Chinese artifacts for me to contemplate

The Rape of Nanking: Ida remained in China during the Japanese invasion and occupation

Send Me the Names: after the war Ida spent the remaining years of her life in Durban, South Africa. In one letter home she wrote a request in passing for the names of those Canadian boys from the region around the village of Highgate who had volunteered to go to Korea to keep the peace before the Korean War broke out

Because She Failed to Attend Her Sister's Anniversary: Ida was never forgiven by some in the family for failing to attend her sister Mara's wedding anniversary

Mu--Not--lament for the lost kingdom of I am: from here on the poems are inspired by my travels in the China, Korea and Thailand. My elder son Dylan married a young woman from Korea and my younger son Sean married a young woman from Thailand, so I have had occasion to travel there. Dylan's spent ten years living in Korea where his two sons were born. Sean's son was born in Canada. The poems in this section under the title *Counting Cranes* received Honourable mention in the Cranberry Tree Press chapbook award

In 2005 John B. Lee was inducted as Poet Laureate of Brantford in perpetuity. The same year he received the distinction of being named Honourary Life Member of The Canadian Poetry Association and The Ontario Poetry Society. In 2007 he was made a member of the Chancellor's Circle of the President's Club of McMaster University and named first recipient of the Souwesto Award for his contribution to literature in his home region of southwestern Ontario and he was named winner of the inaugural Black Moss Press *Souwesto Award* for his contribution to the ethos of writing in Southwestern Ontario. In 2011 he was appointed Poet Laureate of Norfolk County (2011-14) and in 2015 Honourary Poet Laureate of Norfolk County for life and in 2017 he received a Canada 150 Medal from the Federal Government of Canada for "his outstanding contribution to literary development both at home and abroad." A recipient of over eighty prestigious international awards for his writing he is winner of the $10,000 CBC Literary Award for Poetry, the only two time recipient of the People's Poetry Award, and 2006 winner of the inaugural Souwesto Orison Writing Award (University of Windsor). In 2007 he was named winner of the Winston Collins Award for Best Canadian Poem, an award he won again in 2012. He has well-over seventy books published to date and is the editor of seven anthologies including two best-selling works: *That Sign of Perfection*: poems and stories on the game of hockey; and *Smaller Than God*: words of spiritual longing. He co-edited a special issue of *Windsor Review—Alice Munro: A Souwesto Celebration* published in the fall of 2014. His work has appeared internationally in over 500 publications, and has been translated into French, Spanish, Korean and Chinese. He has read his work in nations all over the world including South Africa, France, Korea, Cuba, Canada and the United States. He has received letters of praise from Nelson Mandela,

Desmond Tutu, Australian Poet, Les Murray, and Senator Romeo Dallaire. Called "the greatest living poet in English," by poet George Whipple, he lives in Port Dover, Ontario where he works as a full time author.

Books by John B. Lee

Poems Only A Dog Could Love, (poetry) Applegarth Follies, London, Ontario, 1976 88pp.

Love Among the Tombstones, (poetry) Dogwood Press, Simcoe, Ontario, 1980 80 pp.

Fossils of the Twentieth Century, (poetry) Vesta Publications, Cornwall, Ontario, 1983 75 pp.

Small Worlds, (poetry) Vesta Publications, Cornwall, Ontario, 1986 89 pp.

Hired Hands, (poetry and prose) Brick Books, 1986 85 pp.

Rediscovered Sheep, (poetry) Brick Books, 1987 80 pp.

★The Bad Philosophy of Good Cows, (poetry) Black Moss Press, Windsor, Ontario, 1989 77 pp.

The Hockey Player Sonnets, (poetry) Penumbra Press, 1991 85 pp.

★The Pig Dance Dreams, (poetry) Black Moss Press, 1991 91 pp.

When Shaving Seems Like Suicide, (poetry) Goose Lane Editions, Fredericton, NB, 1992 80 pp.

★The Art of Walking Backwards, (poetry) Black Moss Press, 1993 85 pp.

Variations on Herb, (poetry and prose) Brick Books, London, Ontario, 1993 95 pp.

All the Cats Are Gone, (poetry) Penumbra Press, 1993 77 pp.

★These Are the Days of Dogs and Horses, (poetry) Black Moss Press, 1994 81 pp.

Head Heart Hands Health: A History of 4H in Ontario, (non fiction) Comrie Productions, Peterborough, Ontario, 1994 224 pp.

★The Beatles Landed Laughing in New York, (poetry) Black Moss Press, 1995 79 pp.

★Tongues of the Children, (documentary poetry and prose) Black Moss Press, 1996 115 pp.

*Never Hand Me Anything if I am Walking or Standing, (poetry) Black Moss Press, 1997 91 pp.

*Soldier's Heart, (poetry) Black Moss Press, 1998 75 pp.

*Stella's Journey, (poetry and prose) Black Moss Press, 1999 85 pp.

*Don't Be So Persnickety, (children's verse) Black Moss Press, 2000 55 pp.

*Building Bicycles in the Dark: a practical guide to writing, (non fiction) Black Moss Press, 2001 135 pp.

*The Half-Way Tree: selected poems of John B. Lee, (poetry) Black Moss Press, 2001 150 pp.

In the Terrible Weather of Guns, (documentary poetry and prose) Mansfield Press, Toronto, 2002 97 pp.

The Hockey Player Sonnets: overtime edition (poetry) Penumbra Press, Ottawa, Ontario, 2003 98 pp.

*Totally Unused Heart, (poetry) Black Moss Press, 2003 66 pp.

*The Farm on the Hill He Calls Home, (memoir) Black Moss Press, 2004 155 pp.

*Poems for the Pornographer's Daughter, (poetry and prose) Black Moss Press, 2005 75 pp.

*Godspeed, (documentary poetry and prose) Black Moss Press, 2006 75 pp.

*Left Hand Horses: meditations on influence and the imagination, (essays) Black Moss Press, 2007 115 pp.

*The Place that We Keep After Leaving, (poetry) Black Moss Press, 2008 64 pp.

Island on the Wind-Breathed Edge of the Sea, (poetry) Hidden Brook Press, 2008 75 pp.

Being Human, (poetry) Sunbun Press, 2010 73 pp.

Dressed in Dead Uncles, (poetry) Black Moss Press, 2010 81 pp.

In the Muddy Shoes of Morning, (poetry) Hidden Brook Press, 2010 115 pp.

Sweet Cuba: Three-Hundred Years of Cuban poetry in Spanish and in English translation—John B. Lee and Manuel de Jesus (poetry and prose introduction) (Hidden Brook Press, 2010) 355 pp.

King Joe: A Matter of Treason—the life and times of Joseph Willcocks (1773-September 5, 1814) (popular history in prose) (Heronwood Enterprises, Summer, 2011) 85 pp.

Let Us Be Silent Here (poetry) (Sanbun Publishing, 2012) 85 pp.

You Can Always Eat the Dogs: the hockeyness of ordinary men (prose memoir) (Black Moss Press, 2012) 88 pp.

In This We Hear the Light (poetry and photographs) (Hidden Brook Press, 2013) 84 pp.

Burning My Father, (Black Moss Press, April 2014)

The Full Measure, (fall 2015)

Secret Second Language of the Heart, (Sanbun Publishing, spring, 2016)

The Widow's Land: superstition and farming—a madness of daughters, prose memoir, (forthcoming Black Moss Press, 2016)

These Are the Words (Hidden Brook Press, 2017)

MMXVII (Sanbun Press, 2017)

Beautiful Stupid, (Black Moss Press, 2018)

This is How We See the World, (Hidden Brook Press, 2018)

Chapbooks

To Kill a White Dog, (documentary poem) Brick Books, 1982 25 pp.

The Day Jane Fonda Came to Guelph, (poetry) The Ploughman Press, Whitby, Ontario, 1996 35 pp.

What's in a Name: the pursuit of George Peacock, Namesake of Peacock Point, (essay) Dogwood Press, Brantford, Ontario, 1996 15 pp.

In a Language with No Word For Horses, (documentary poems) above/ground press, Ottawa, Ontario, 1997 25 pp.

The Echo of Your Words Has Reached Me, (poetry) Mekler & Deahl, Hamilton, Ontario, 1998 20 pp.

An Almost Silent Drumming: the South Africa poems, (poetry) Cranberry Tree Press, Windsor, Ontario, 2001 33 pp.

Thirty-Three Thousand Shades of Green, (poetry) Leaf Press, Lantzville, BC, 2004 35 pp.

Though Their Joined Hearts Drummed Like Larks, (documentary poetry) Passion Among the Cacti Press, Kitchener, Ontario, 2004 22 pp.

Bright Red Apples of the Dead, (poetry) Pooka Press, BC, 2004 25 pp.

*How Beautiful We Are, (poetry) Souwesto Orion Prize, Black Moss Press, 2006 45 pp.

But Where Were the Horses of Evening, (poetry) Serengeti Press, 2007 35 pp.

Let Light Try All the Doors, Rubicon Press, (poetry) fall 2009 35 pp.

One Leaf in the Breath of the World, (poetry) Beret Days Press, 2009 35 pp.

Adoration of the Unnecessary, (poetry) Beret Days Press, 2015

Editor

*That Sign of Perfection: From Bandy Legs to Beer Legs (poems and stories on the game of hockey), (anthology) Black Moss Press, 1995

*Losers First: poems and stories on game and sport, (anthology) Black Moss Press, 1999

*I Want to Be the Poet of Your Kneecaps: poems of quirky romance, (anthology) Black Moss Press, 1999

*Following the Plough: poems and stories on the land, (anthology) Black Moss Press, 2000

*Henry's Creature: poems and stories on the automobile, (anthology co-edited with Roger Bell) Black Moss Press, 2000

*Smaller Than God: words of spiritual longing, (anthology co-edited with Brother Paul Quenon) Black Moss Press, 2001

*Body Language: a head-to-toe anthology, (anthology) Black Moss Press, 2003

Witness: anthology of war poetry, (anthology) Serengeti Press, Mississauga, Ontario, 2004

Bonjour Burgundy, (anthology) Mosaic Press, 2008

*Under the Weight of Heaven, (anthology) Black Moss Press, 2008

*Tough Times: an anthology of essays on the state of the arts in tough economic times, edited by John B. Lee (Black Moss Press, 2010)

*Decabration: the tenth anniversary anthology of The Ontario Poetry Society, Beret Days Books, 2011

When the Full Moon Comes: writing from Santiago de Cuba (Hidden Brook Press, 2012)

An Unfinished War: poems and stories on the War of 1812 (Black Moss Press, 2012)

Beyond the Seventh Morning (Sandcrab, 2012)

Window Fishing: the night we caught Beatlemania, (Hidden Brook Press, 2014) second edition 2015, extended play edition 2016

Alice Munro: A Souwesto Celebration, (edited by J.R. (Tim) Struthers and John B. Lee, (Windsor Review, Fall, 2014)

*my work has been published internationally in over 500 anthologies, journals, magazines

Work-in-progress

Documentary poems on the life of missionary in China Ida Wight (Mosaic Press, 2019)
Moths That Drink the Tears of Sleeping Birds, (Black Moss Press, 2019)

And I'm am currently working on an anthology

A Bed Too Big for Both of Us